Absolutely Random Stories for Random People (That Means YOU!)
Copyright 2019 by Mabela Press
Written by Erica De Bruin, Madison Hol, Eli Hoksbergen and
Laurey Johnson in conjunction with Kari Litscher DeBruin

All rights reserved. No portion of this book may be reproduced, stored in a retrieval system or transmitted in any form or by any means - electronic, mechanical, photocopy, recording, scanning or other - except for brief quotations in critical review or articles, without the prior written permission of the publisher.

Published in Oskaloosa, Iowa by Mabela Press. Mabela Press is an imprint of Mabela Press.
ISBN: 978-0-9995544-2-5

Foreword

Four weeks.
That's the amount of time we had for our book elective. Four weeks!
We met, discussed, organized and then went for it: a published book.

This group of students has impressed me. While most of the stories collected on these pages were part of our Creative Writing class, several of them have been written specifically for this project. Their dreams of being published authors have now become a reality.

This incredible group of junior high students not only wrote this book together, but they also served as their own editors and publishers.
Is it perfect? Of course not.
But it is it a dream achieved? Absolutely.

Congratulations Erica, Madi, Eli and Laurey.
I am blessed, thankful, and humbled (not to mention exhausted!) to have been a part of this. I am very proud of all of you.
Ms. Kari DeBruin

Thank You's
& Dedications

We would like to thank our teacher, Kari DeBruin,

for making this book possible and teaching us everything on the way.

Eli -

This is for my Grandma, who was the best. Also Mom who always loves me, my Dad who always teaches me and my very important chicken, Filay, who taught me how to talk to grownups. I would also like to thank my siblings who showed me what a tragedy really is.

Madison -

I'd like to thank my wonderful mom, dad, and sister

for always helping me to do my best.

Laurey -

This is for my mom, who always pushed me to do better, my smart dad,

and my three peasant sisters.

Table of Contents

Fables
The Pig and the Goat	6
The Cheetah and the Koala	8
The Dog and the Cat	11
The Bear and the Beaver	13

Tragedies
How Animals Die	18
Ouch	19
The Two Best Friends	23
The Bright Blue Flower	25

Comedies
Junior High	31
The Snow Cat	33
The Day in the Life of a Pair of Tennis Shoes	35
Merry Christmouse	37

Fairy Tales
Big Green Riding Shoes	41
The Non-princess and the Hot Pink Yoga Ball	44
Snow White and the 14 Giants	47
Sleeping Beauty's Lost Prince	50

A Little Longer Stories
The Better Grinch	59
Why You Should Never Play Hide and Seek	61
A Dent in the Jungle	69

Random stories
Monopoly	85
The Legend of Drakon	87
The Girl and her Goose Egg	90
The Door in the Wall	92

Fables

The Pig and the Goat

by Erica De Bruin

Pig was walking down the road when he saw a cornfield. The corn looked delicious. Pig was eating some corn when he saw Goat.

"Hey Goat, I see you've got some nice corn in your hand."

"It seems I do," said Goat. Goat loved corn, it was his favorite food.

"You know I saw a nice field filled with delicious corn just a mile away," said Pig.

So Goat dropped all his corn and went to find the cornfield. When Pig got all done eating his corn he started heading home. He came across a hole in the middle of the road.

"Help me I've fallen in this hole!" screeched Goat.

Pig pretended he didn't hear Goat and wandered home. The next morning Pig went back to the cornfield. He came across the same hole Goat had fallen into yesterday, but he wasn't in the hole anymore. When he had gotten to the cornfield he saw Goat picking corn of the stalk. Pig decided to go over to Goat he tricked him again that day.

A week went by and Pig kept tricking Goat. This went on for the rest of their lives. Up until Pig got taken to get butchered.

Moral- Trickery does not end well.

The Cheetah and the Koala

by Eli Hoksbergen

Once, there was a cheetah. He was very proud because he could run twice as fast as anyone else within a hundred miles. One day the cheetah saw someone new he didn't know. It was a koala. He chuckled. When he went over and started a conversation. The cheetah asked, "Where are you from?"

"Bulgeria" (BULG-aria)

"Oh… so what do you like to do there in BULGeria?"

"Oh, mostly sleep and eat, I *LOVE* eating."

"What," exclaimed the cheetah, "no sports!?!"

"No, why would we want sports?"

"You **Monster**, you **Vagabond**, *YOU HAVE NO SPOTS, AND YOU DON'T EVEN WANT THEM!?!"*

"No why would we want them? Sleeping and eating are much easier."

"YOU LAZY BO-BO HEAD."

"How rude can you get!?!"

"Can you get lazier!?!"

"You jerk!"

"I'LL SHOW YOU!!!"

"I challenge you to a race!"

"I ACCEPT, AND MAY YOU LOSE, YOU LOSER!"

"When should we start?"

"TONIGHT, AT MIDNIGHT!"

"Ok, see-"

*"Ah, but wait. This race will be on **motorcycles down the dead animals doom path.** I'm not as dumb as the hare that raced the Tortoise."*

"Um…. ok, but, but, but…"

"EXCELLENT, now that we understand each other--"

"Let's go to bed" said the tired koala.

Later when koala was in bed, he was mad.

"I was going to take a Lamborghini, and beat him so bad, but now he outsmarted me."

That night, he climbed up the hill in terror. **Moral of the story: Use your wits.**

The Dog and the Cat

by Madison Hol

Once there was a dog and a cat, they were best friends and they did everything together. One day they were going to the park, they ran into Dog's enemies and they were teasing him. Cat called out "Stop!" The leader of the group looked at her and said, "Why? Does Dog need a cat to protect him?"

"While they were talking the dog who was holding Dog let go and Dog got free and yelled, "Run, Cat, before they get you!"

Then Dog turned and said to the dogs, "Thank you for the wonderful time. I hope that I do not see you again soon, good bye!"

Later that day Cat meet with Dog at his house.

"What are you doing Dog? "asked Cat

"Oh, I am just cleaning my wounds. Those dogs are really mean, try not to get tangled with them."

"Okay, but if you get caught I will bite and claw them until they let you go."

"Thanks Cat, I appreciate that very much."

Moral of the Story: Do not let others bully you, and if you see someone getting bullied try to help them the best that you can.

The Bear and the Beaver

by Laurey Johnson

Once upon a time, there was a beaver that lived in a beautiful dam, in a clean river. He had plenty of food, and he always shared with others. In this same forest, there was a grizzly bear. He lived far away from the river and was very selfish. The only reason he had plenty of food was because he stole it from others.

One day this bear happened to meet this beaver.

"Who are you?" the kind beaver asked.

"I am the greatest grizzly in the entire forest. I am hungry and I need food." the bear growled.

"Of course, come to my dam and I can share some of my food with you."

As the beaver led the bear to his dam, the bear decided to steal all the beaver's food when he wasn't looking.

"Here's my beautiful dam." the beaver said, when they arrived.

"What a beautiful dam you have." the bear replied slyly. "I shall like to go inside and see it."

"Ok." said the beaver.

The grizzly bear's eyes grew wide when he saw the spoils of the beaver. *I will come back tonight to steal everything*, thought the bear.

When the day had passed, and all was still, the bear crept into the beaver's dam. He crept into the house quickly, because some storm clouds had crept in the sky as well. The beaver was snoring loudly, making the bear's job easier. He ate the beaver's food very quickly. The bear was now very groggy from his feasting, so he shouted in a loud voice, "I have never eaten as much as this! I will never have to eat again!"

At this the beaver woke up and saw the bear. He screamed to the bear, "What have you done? Now many animals in the forest can't eat because of you!"

"I don't care," said the bear, "they can all die if they want!" Just as he finished saying this, lightning struck the dam. The fire started almost instantly.

"Quick get out of here!" the beaver yelled as he swam out.

"Wait!" the bear said. "You've got to help me! I'm too big to run fast!"

The beaver couldn't help him. The bear tried to run, but the dam collapsed and the bear was no more.

The morale of the story is: "the more greed, the less speed."

Tragedies

How Animals Die

by Erica De Bruin

The goat died. The pig died. The turkey died. The dog died. The cat died. The monkey died. The lamb died. The squirrel died. The giraffe died. The bird died. The lion died. The peacock died. The tiger died. The chipmunk died. The cow died. The alligator died. The seal died. The wolf died. The polar bear died. The bunny died. The rooster died. The horse died. The owl died. The ant died. The spider died. The fish died. The zebra died. The rhino died. The water buffalo and the elephant died. The sea turtle died. All the animals died because of pollution or getting hit by a car. Either way it was most likely from a human. Or it could have been by another animal.

Ouch

by Eli Hoksbergen

Once in Los Angeles, California, there lived a family of sixteen children. They were not healthy, happy children, but rich thieves, and just plan jerks. They robbed wherever they went, and then destroyed everything in the place they just robbed. But the reason everyone hated them was because they burned the stuff they stole and that they could ask their parents for it and they would get it instantly.

One day while they were robbing a skyscraper, the oldest child, Frederica; messing around on the stolen phone, walked off the top of the skyscraper texting. The other siblings didn't notice Frederica was missing until their father screamed, "you must go find your sister or instead of soft-serve ice cream, you will get 1 bucket of ice cream!!!" the remaining children screamed in horror. "No soft-serve ice cream!?!" one wailed.

They immediately rushed out of the house to find their lost sister. They rushed to the robbed skyscraper, only to find it surrounded by police. One of the youngest sisters, Olga, whom they nicknamed "old guy" thought it would be a good idea to talk to the police, and ask if they had found their sister. As soon as the police spotted her, they ceased Olga, tried her, and then when found guilty, put her in a metal cylinder, the poured in cement up to her neck before trying her. (They did this because they didn't want her to escape.) She was condemned to the rest of her life in prison and her family never saw her again and the grandma said, "good riddance, she was always so loud!"

Meanwhile, at the skyscraper, the older children climbed to the top of a neighboring skyscraper and looked down at the street for their missing sister. They soon found clue quickly and ran down only to find a pancake. Billy quietly whispered to Pumpkin that he thought that the pancake was actually their sister, Frederica. Billy was right. They ran home to tell their father, but on the way there, Pumpkin, one of the boy carrying Frederica, was crushed by her enormous weight when the Billy dropped her on him after tripping. Almost immediately after, Billy tripped and fell off their family's many private cliffs.

Many people in California and around it were experiencing similar quakes. Scientists dug out the old theory of California floating away and the warned they president that California was going to float away. "Bah," said the president. "You're crazy. What did we ever do to California that would make it want to float away? I didn't think that the last 80% purchase tax was that bad." So the president wouldn't listen.

While they were thinking about who to tell next, people already knew California would be floating away. There was a 300-meter-deep by 10-meter-long chasm between California and Oregon, Nevada, Arizona, and Baja California, Mexico.

"I am Sunny Glamor reporting live for Sparkly Today here at the city of Primm. Here on Sparkle Today, we have the facts, the live feed, and the perfectly gelled hair.

I am at the city of Primm, Nevada, just up highway 15 from the California state border, and what a mess it is. There is a huge crevice in between California and the land neighboring it. Oh-aaaaaaaa, California is floating away! 10 feet- no 20- no 50 feet in just 10 seconds."

California really was floating away; it was already 5 miles in just 10 hours.

Back at the manor, things were going less smoothly. It had already sunk more than ten feet into the water and sharks had started to circle it.

"California has floated away." Declared the President. "It must have decided to secede, to break away from the union. I have decided that we will not let it. Even now, nuclear weapons are being prepared for dropping." "We will not let them leave without a fight." The president screeched. "Wait, I have just received intelligence that California is sinking. Its inhabitants must have heard about our nuclear weapons. Its inhabitants are being eaten by sharks. I think that their escape has turned on them. They are all dead." And the nuclear weapons are going to explode in 18- 7- 3- 9- I hate counting. 0 already. Hey, that means I'm going to explode too. Uh-oh that is going to ruin my lunch plan.

The Two Best Friends

by Madison Hol

Once there was two girls and they were best friends. One was a Jew and her name was Anna; the other was German, her name was Anne. There was one problem though, it was 1939 (if you are up on your history you would know that that is during WW2!) And as you know, during WW2 the Germans were persecuting the Jews and that is a big problem considering that Anna is a Jew and Anne is a German. Well one day Anne came home from school and her mom told her that she could not play with Anna any more. She was so mad that she yelled at her mom and ran to her room. Then she went over to Anna's house and told her that they are not allowed to play together and they will play together secretly.

Anna asked who told her that they could not play together and Anne told her that it was her mother. Anne said that it was because she was German and Anne was a Jew. Later that day Anne learned that Anna had disappeared. Anne was so sad that she blamed her mother for over hearing their plan to play together secretly. Her mother said that

Anna was a Jew and that Jews were bad people and they had to be taken away. That made Anne even angrier, she ran out to find Anna and join her and/or save her. They never ever came back. Anne's mother felt so bad about not stopping her daughter before she ran away. She also felt bad about not letting Anne and Anna play together.

The Bright Blue Flower

By Laurey Jonson

Avery shivered. She was so cold. The winter had been harsh, almost as harsh as the war. The biggest war the world has ever seen: World War 3, 3001.

Avery was a 12-year old girl. She had auburn hair and fair skin. She was 6'0 and very skinny. Her dad, Will Finley, had been drafted for the American army. And her mother, Martha… She was missing. But she was going to find her.

The sky was dank and dark. She pulled sweatshirt tightly around her face. She walked back to her old home. She looked around to make sure no one was there, and went in.

As soon as her mother had disappeared, she was kicked out of her home. (The war is so expensive that many people got taxed out of their homes.) Her home was spectacular. It had a large entryway, furnished with an antique rocking chair, a Swiss clock, and a mahogany armoire.

The living room was full of priceless items, such as a grandfather clock from the 2000s, a Persian rug from the Middle East, and a life size family portrait. The rest of the house was equally glamorous. Each room had a precious decor item from around the world. There were Russian nesting dolls, an Australian didgeridoo, a sombrero, stuffed bear carpet, and so much more.

Avery sighed, remembering that it was no more. The intruders sold most everything that had belonged to her family. Avery grew angry. She was about to march into the house, when she realized she had more important things to.

She snuck to the back of the house, and listened. A few seconds later she heard a woman scream, "Get that mouse! Oh get it before it gets to my clothes!"

"Oh hush up!" a man replied in a gruff voice. "It won't take me long to kill it. Just sit back and relax, let me do my thing."
The man grabbed a piece of wood and smashed the mouse with a whack.

That is disgusting. Avery thought. The man was now carrying the mouse, with the woman following behind him. Once they left Avery went inside. She looked through the living room, looking for clues as to where her mother might be. All she found was her dad's old sock.

Then she combed through the kitchen with the same amount of luck. (She found a box of spaghetti, for those who are curious.) She finally went up to her parents' room. She looked under every pillow, through every drawer, and every closet. She lay on the bed in despair. She couldn't find anything that belonged to either of her parents. She stared at the ceiling, lost. That's when she noticed something was there. She sat upright, and saw a brilliant blue flower, hanging from above. She grabbed a chair and stood on it. She grabbed the flower with ease. When she inspected it she found a note written on the back of it. It said, "You'll find me where the trees haven't fallen, Mom."

Footsteps echoed from downstairs. There was no way Avery could make it out without being seen. She needed a plan.
"Why did we have to take a dead mouse so far away?" the woman whined.

"You didn't have to go with me." the man answered. "Besides, I didn't want you to complain about the reek of the dead thing."

"Those things stink when they die! The nerve of the little beasts." the woman shuddered.

Avery quietly took he sweatshirt off. She cracked opened the window. She put her sweatshirt on the power line. 3,2,1… She jumped, and went soaring downwards. When she was at the bottom she let go. She landed safely, and then took off running. She knew exactly where her mother wanted her to go. It was the state park. She dodged traffic, ignored street lights, ran into people, but she didn't care.

When she arrived at the park, no one was there. She crept in, and began her search. She went to the main campgrounds, and found nothing. She went to the camp store. Nothing. She went through the trails. Nothing at all.

She lay down on a bench and fell asleep. When she woke up, she saw a blurry figure staring at her. She dashed away, hoping that the police wouldn't find her. She stopped, realizing that she knew who it was.

"Mother!" Avery, yelled in delight.

"Aver-"

A bomb dropped from the sky with a loud crash. Avery backed up just in time to avoid it. Her mother wasn't so lucky. Avery screamed, only to realize, it made no sound. She had no clue what to do. All she could do was run. She ran. Back past the people, past the street signs, past a big army truck, BAAM! Avery was no more.

5 years later...

Will Finley let out a sigh of relief. The war was over. America was on the winning side, celebrating victory. He was so excited to see his wife and sweet Avery…

As he was driving home, he noticed a memorial. It showed a little girl crying. Her resemblance to Avery was eerie. She was also holding a blue flower. It looked like his wife's.

He rushed to get home. He flung open the door, but no one was there. All he saw was a note on the dining table saying, "Your wife and daughter have deceased." He fell his knees. "They're gone."

Comedies

Junior High
by Erica De Bruin

Once upon a long, long, time ago is definitely not how this story is going to begin. Let's start over. Five years ago it was the first day of ugh junior high. The first day of junior high was a NIGHTMARE let me tell you. First I actually had to wake up! Second my annoying brother took the last bagel so I had to eat toast, yuck. Third I had nothing to wear. I am very picky on what I look like. Fourth I had to go to SCHOOL! Dun, dun, dun. Fifth I had to start the day off with science! Sixth I had to do PE. While I was running her 9 laps and I'll say that again 9 whole laps. I think my PE teacher is trying to kill us. Then I had to do 200 jump ropes and here comes the really embarrassing part my pants fell down and the whole class started to laugh and point at my rainbow unicorn underwear. I know what you're thinking what's a junior high student doing wearing rainbow unicorn is. The answer is my mother chose it. After PE I had to got to go to lunch. Which as everyone knows is the best part of the day. Lunch today was Mexican straw hats. BEST LUNCH EVER. The bad part though was that mine was cold and I didn't get very much. After lunch I told the nurse I didn't feel good, so I go to go home. Yes, I get to go home finally after all my embarrassment. When I got home I went to my room and took a two-hour nap. I was very tired.

The Snow Cat

by Eli Hoksbergen

I glared. The snow cat stared back with unblinking rocks; I mean eyes. Through the frost covered windows the snow cat glared at me. Cruel master, making me an enemy to fight. My master didn't care about me. I was really lucky to get food three times a week. My Mean Master always kicked me, and ignored me, and now, now of all times his grandchildren have made a torture device, and I can't even destroy it. Curse you, see-through wall!!!!!

I crawled over to my bed and laid my soft head down to try to get some rest. It never came. Moments after I had laid down, my Mean Master's grandchildren tramped in took one look at me then picked me up and carried me out in the bone chilling, icy, jagged, accursed wind. Through me down right next to the snow cat and went back inside, firmly closing the door behind them.

I was alone with my mortal foe, the SNOWCAT OF DOOM!!! I mean the snow cat. I hope it is not of doom or I will be toast with white jam.

I glared at the snow cat. It glared back at me. I slowly approached. I pounced. It dodged with a speed I had never seen. When I look back at it now all I can remember is a blur of high speed attacks; the snow cat was VERY, VERY vicious. I remember one time the snow cat had me pinned down but in my own clever genius I just managed to escape the snow cat's clutches. I won. I think. Probably.

(snow cat's perspective now of the fight events)

The amazing children that had built me tortured my mortal enemy, the CAT OF DOOM. I hope it is not as hostile as that but I am not sure. He stumbled over to me, and jumped at me, but missed by a foot. He must have been crazed. He jumped at me 1,000nds of times, but missed every time. Once he hit my arm and it fell of and trapped itself under it. Once he finally managed to get out from under it he tried to knock me down, but kept missing, after 5 hours, the wonderful children can back and grabbed him and took him back in. I won. Positively.

A Day in the Life of a Pair of Tennis Shoes

by Madison Hol

"It smells so bad in here! Let me out! Did she even wash her feet last night? Did she change her socks? I think that I am the only shoe that has an owner with such stinky feet!

"The first thing that always happens to me in the day is when Allie puts her stinky feet in my hole. She pulls on my tongue, she steps on my heel, and if she is in a real hurry she stuffs her feet in me and runs."

"I just remembered that the only time that Allie wears me is when she has PE. That means that she has PE today! That is NOT good at all. When she has PE I am squished and squashed. If you ever have the chance to try it, you should. It is the worst feeling ever and if you do it, do not do it again.

"Allie rides the bus home in the afternoon and it is the worst thing ever. I get stepped on by people who I don't even know and I don't think that they even go to the same school as us (Allie even sometimes kicks). I hate the bus. When we finally get home my day is not over until Allie is done doing her chores, which consist of playing with the dog, collecting eggs, feeding chickens, giving chickens water.

"When my day is finally over I am put in the closet. I don't understand how the flip-flops handle being worn every day. I can barely stand it when I get sweated in."

"Hey, tennis shoes, how was your day?" called the sweat shirt. "I had a terrible day. I was sweated in."

Merry Christmouse

by Laurey Johnson

I barely made it under the table. As a mouse I almost never find a moment of rest. I'm Harley, the family's mouse. It's Christmas and the Jameson family is in pretty good cheer. They decorated my ledge above the fireplace, and also they put a tree there to make me more at home. The only problem is that the wreath is blocking my hole. I tried to explain my problem to them, but they wouldn't listen. M0m just took the broom and started whacking it all over the place. That's why I'm under the table.

I tried putting one paw out from under the table. WHACK! Apparently someone's still salty that I made a good argument. While Mom's screaming her salty head off, I dashed under the tree. She saw me make it and screamed, "George, it's going to ruin our tree! Get it away! Get it away!"

Some bonehead was playing Christmas music while I raced up to the top of the tree. George was gaining on me. He kept smashing ornaments trying to get to me so it sounded like, "Da, da da smash, da, da, da, da, da, da, da." I made to the top of the tree and I was trapped. George grabbed the top of the tree. "I've got you now!" he screamed.

I bit his hand, and he let go. I went flying through the air. I saw Mom; she fainted. A breeze flew in and moved the wreath. "Don't let Harley get in his hole-" Whomp. Nailed it! Safe at last.

Fairy Tales

Big Green Riding Shoes

by Erica De Bruin

There once was a girl named Polly. Who lived in a little cottage on the outskirts of town. Her mother told her to go and give the freshly made cookies to her grandfather. Polly's grandfather lived all the way on the other side of town. She started her journey as soon as she had put on her favorite pair of green tennis shoes. On her way she wanted to stop at her friend's parents' bakery to see if her friend was there, but she decided that she better get to her grandfather's house. Polly had to go on the subway to just get halfway to her grandfather's house. She got on the subway and took her seat. She had just taken her seat when she realized her green tennis shoes were all dirty. Thankfully she had brought her backpack with her. She pulled out a pack of Clorox wipes and started wiping her shoes off. By the time she had to get off her shoes were nice and green again. She was just started into the city when her friend saw her and stopped her. "Hey what's up?" her friend asked her.

"I'm headed to my grandpa's to bring him some cookies." said Polly.

"OK I'll let you get headed there." said her friend.

Polly left and was headed on her way. When she got to her grandpa's house the door was unlocked. That was very unusual because her grandpa was a very cautious man. Polly walked in and found him in his bed. He said he felt sick so he was resting. I said that I would just put the cookies on the counter and to feel better. She left and locked the door behind her, but something didn't feel right. She felt worried about her grandpa, so she decided to stay and take care of him. Polly unlocked the door and when she walked in there he was eating her cookies. There was something strange about him. Like how his hair looked longer and how his ears looked pointier. She walked over and stood behind him until he turned around. When he turned around she spooked him. It turns out it wasn't really him! Polly quickly ran over to the phone and called the police. The man was too quick he stole the phone out of Polly's hand and said, "Your grandpa's in the bedroom. He really is sick. I'm your grandpa's friend I was just taking care him."

"Oh. I'm sorry." said Polly. Polly went into the bedroom to see her grandpa. Her grandpa looked like he was a little pale, but he was going to be fine. After getting to know each other Polly and her grandpa's friend named Bob became best friends.

The Non-Princess and the Hot Pink Yoga Ball

by Eli Hoksbergen

Once upon a time, there was a prince whose parents wanted their sons to only Mary a true princess. As a result, whenever a pretty girl came over that the prince thought was nice, they piled 23 *million* mattresses on top of a pea. Ha-ha, got you. They really only pilled 7 mattresses, 10 blankets, and 6 pillows. Then they waited until morning and asked the princess if she had slept good. She always said yes for two reasons. 1 princess always had to be **SUPER** polite even when it was such a dumb lie that everyone in the room fell over laughing. 2. They really had sept amazing, and everyone knows that real princesses don't tell lies. 3. They must exaggerate and be descriptive. All the other ones just said that slept fine. They should have said they slept gorgeously, and did not stir even once during the night.

One night a super duper ugly girl came to the castle steps and raked her nails on the portcullis, making and horrible screeching. It woke up everyone in the castle up. But once they had given her some new clothes and she had washed, she was beautiful. Her hair was a river of gold. Her eyes were fountains of joy that sparkled with humor of settled down into the wells of thought. The prince fell in love almost immediately. He just stares at her enough. But she didn't act like a princess. She ate very messily. She couldn't sit still. She didn't cut up her bites into precisely 3 milligram bites. When the girl was getting tired, the prince's mother put a single frozen pea under her bed. But the prince, in love with the girl, say that both his parents were talking, he sneaked into the girl's bedroom, and put his favorite yoga ball, the hot pink one, under her bed.

The next morning, when the queen asked how the girl had slept, she had quite an exciting answer. "When I first lay down my belly button was 3 feet above my head. But when I rolled over, I started bouncing around my room, and next thing I know, I wake up with all my blankets, mattresses, and pillows on my head.

Then the parents discussed her tall tail, but decided she hadn't slept well enough and so they let the prince marry her. And they lived happily ever after, even though the prince didn't marry a real princess.

Snow White and the 14 Giants

by Madison Hol

You may know Snow White as a kind, sweet girl. Well, in this story she is not. This story is just about the complete opposite of the story that you think it will be.

In this story, Snow White is not very kind or sweet, the Evil Stepmother is not so evil, and let's say that the dwarfs are not very much like dwarfs. I would say that they are more like giants (they are 9' 10'') they do not fit in their house very well, so they have to crawl everywhere that they want to go in their house.

This story starts like any other princess fairytale, but it does not stay like that. It starts with a widower and his daughter, but this daughter is not the nicest girl in the kingdom, in fact, she is the meanest (she was spoiled as a result of being motherless). She says that she is the most important person because her dad is the king. All the other girls think that she is the nastiest, meanest girl in the whole kingdom.

One day Snow White's father decided to remarry. He married the nicest, kindest woman in the kingdom. Snow White hated that woman so much that she decided to run away into **The Black Forest.** No one liked The **Black Forest** because there were rumors that there was a big dragon in the forest (there actually was a dragon in the forest, but it was the Giant's pet).

The stepmother (whose name was actually Polly) kept saying that this was all her fault. The king kept saying that she was right.

Meanwhile, while Snow White was wandering in the forest some giants came up to her.

"Hello there, Madam, you look a little lost. May we be of any assistance?" asked the tallest.

"Yes, would you like to come to our house? Or would you like to keep wandering around the forest like you are now?" said the shortest.

"Oh, yes, I would like that very much. Thank you," said Snow White, while thinking very rude things.

"Wonderful," said the tallest again.

When they got to the giant's house Snow White asked, "Where will my room be. Please show it to me quickly and you all may be on your way."

The giants were all thinking that Snow White was very bossy, and thinking that they did not have a room for her.

"Please do not boss us around like that or we will kick you out."

"Fine, do what you want with me. My father will come and save me. Of course, it will be after he leaves that evil witch."

"What evil witch? There is no evil witch in the palace that I have heard of," asked the giant that everyone forgets.

"Well, everyone in the palace and in town say that she is very kind and sweet and gentle, and beautiful, but in my opinion she is the rudest, meanest, and ugliest person in the whole kingdom."

In the end all was well. Snow White went back home, and learned to be nice, even to the very nice evil witch.

Sleeping Beauty's Lost Prince

by Laurey Johnson

Once upon a time, in land somewhere in the distance, there lived a king and queen. Their names were Farlo and Cecilia. They were having an awesome day, because it was their princess' first birthday party. Her name was Catherine, but everyone called her Carley. They invited everyone from everywhere. They even invited King James that lives further away. He brought his wife, Melanie, and 6-year old son, named Rupert.

This was the best party of them all. The party had been themed woodland creatures. The banners were filled with cuddly rabbits, busy ants, and chubby bears. It was baby paradise.

"Dad, why does this place look like a unicorn barfed it?" whined Rupert.

"Hush up, my boy! It is not nice to criticize the baby Carley."

"But it's so lame! Can I just go home and play Fortnite?"

"Absolutely not! If change your attitude, I'll royal spanking."

"Fine."

Meanwhile the rest of people were talking calmly amongst themselves. The main topic of conversation, was of course, Carley. They were all excited for the magical gifting ceremony. The magical gifting ceremony was when the royal fairies gave the next heir a gift that only they could give.

"Attention everyone!" yelled Farlo. "The fairies have arrived for the gifting ceremony!" Everybody rushed to the center of the room. They were all impatient for it to start.

The first fairy said, "I Callie, will give Carley the gift of good looks, and the love of Italian food." A picture of shopping bags, and spaghetti appeared on her forehead. Then they faded.

The next fairy happily said, "I Laura, give you the gift of immense kindness. This is what she will be known for." A picture of a heart appeared and faded as before.

The next fairy gave her patience, and the next grace. Just as the last fairy was about to speak, a cloud of black smoke filled the room. Out of that smoke came the most evil being in the land. It was Larissa.

"Nice party you have, Farlo." she said casually. "But tell me, why wasn't I invited?" She was inches away from Farlo's face.

He stammered, "Because, I, I, I knew you would bring smoke along. A- a- and you would diss- disrespect m-me."

"Well, maybe I wouldn't if you had invited me." she replied coldly.

"Just leave! You yourself said you weren't invited," he yelled at her.

"Not until I give your precious daughter a gift from."

The room was dead quiet. As Larissa approached Carley, her mouth bent into a wicked grin.

"Little brat, I give you only what you deserve. If you take only but a bite of garlic on your 18th birthday, you shall die!" with that she cackled and disappeared, filling the room with more smoke.
The room was filled with nervous chatter. Why would she die by garlic? How could the prevent this. Would garlic be banned forever?

"Everyone!" the last fairy cried with a loud voice. Everyone stopped talking at once. "I think I know how to fix this a bit!"

"Tell us! Tell us!" queen Cecilia wailed.

"While I can't totally get rid of the spell," the fairy said, "I can change it. This is how I'll do it. The garlic will not kill Carley, it will only put her, and the rest of the kingdom, in a deep sleep. She can only be woken up if a prince kisses her. That, my sweet child, is my gift to you." "Thank you." the king said to the fairy. Then he addressed the crowd, "Since the garlic is what will be the headline tragedy on social media, I will now make it illegal. Anyone found with even garlic salt, will be given ten years in jail."

Soon, all garlic in the land was either burned, or dumped in the ocean. It could not be found anywhere. Farlo was satisfied, and decided that it was safe to keep Carley at the castle.

Carley grew up with the gifts that the fairies had given her. She always got the most like on Instagram, because of her beauty, she ate the most Italian food, she was the kindest, and most graceful person ever. The only thing she lacked where brains. She was so dumb, that if you asked her what 2 plus 2 is, she would say 3. No matter how many teachers she had, she could never figure out school work. Even YouTube did nothing for her.

Meanwhile, in another kingdom, Rupert grew up too. Even though he wasn't as handsome as Hugh Jackman, he was very smart, He was so smart, that he could tell you the square root of pi without even pulling out a calculator. He was so smart, that his father had him co-rule the kingdom.

On the day of Carley's 18th birthday, she decided to go out to eat by herself. Her parents figured nothing would go wrong, since garlic had been banned. They were wrong,

She met Rupert on the way and said, "Hello random stranger. How are doing?"

He replied, "Oh I'm just doing some boring errands. How about you?"

"I was going out for Italian food. Do you want to come with me?"

"Sure, I have nothing important to do."

Together they went, a random couple to a random Italian restaurant. They sat at a table for two and talked about their lives. Carley ordered spaghetti, and Rupert had the same.

What the two of them didn't know, was that Larissa, had used her magic to disguise herself as a waitress. She put garlic salt in the salt shaker.

"I recommend that you add some salt to your dish." said Larissa.

"I'll put that on for you." Rupert said cheerfully.

Carley took a bite of spaghetti. "Oh my goodness! This is the best-" just then she collapsed on the floor. Larissa quickly vanished from the scene. Rupert rushed to her side. Her smelled her breath and shouted, "I think she's eaten garlic!"

The whole town panicked. They knew that soon they would also fall into a deep sleep. The put everything into storage and went straight to their homes. Carley was rushed to the castle. As soon as she laid her head on her pillow, the whole kingdom froze. Nothing moved at all. Not even the sun moved. Blades of grass were set in one position.

Rupert, having been there at the gifting ceremony, remembered what had to be done to save the kingdom. He went to the castle, but was confronted by Larissa.

She said to him, "I will let you pass, but only if you answer this question correctly. What is the square root of pi?"

"That's easy." said Rupert. "It can't be simplified. There is no solution"

"Wait really?" said the amazed Larissa. "All my life I thought there was an answer! You're smart. Do you want to come to my house and discuss math?"

"But, what about Carley?"

"She can't even figure out 2 plus 2. Do you really want to live with a girl like that?"

"You're right." replied Rup Some other prince will rescue her. I don't have to do anything. Let's go to your house. I can teach you trigonometry."

They left, leaving the kingdom behind. Another prince did not come to rescue her. She lied there forever. All hope was gone.

A Little Longer Stories

The Better Grinch

by Eli Hoksbergen

"Oh I HATE this time of year," said the green, hairy GRINCH to his dog max. Max happily jumped up and down in anticipation of whatever the master wanted with him. "Today, Max, on this glorious day, we are going to steal, wait for it............ Christmas from the smiths. Those ugly, wealthy, penny pinchers, the smiths.

Now down in their huge mansion, smiths were putting up their glorious, expensive decorations. They had already gotten their Christmas tree and their lights, but they still had loads of others, and the food still had to be made.

Up in their mountain hideout, the Grinch harness up Max and rode off on their mission to steal Christmas from the smiths. And as they rode down the mountain into the dark cover of dusk they drew near the mansion of the Smiths when they had finally pulled up.

Crunch, crunch, crunch, went the snow making its repetitive noise and the grinch walked up to the smith's side window.

As he looked in, all he saw was the Christmas tree, so he moved to the next window, the only lights that were on were the tree's and the decorations.

He slipped to the front door cracked it, and slipped inside. The hall was full of decorations, even more than he saw from the window. Ha quickly gathered it all up in 89 bags, loaded them on his sleigh, and took off into the night to use them to decorate this own cave.

When the smiths woke the next morning, they gasped and fainted at their loss. "It was so expensive" cried the daughter. "Oh no, now we will have to buy all the stuff again." the Father said. "Eh, it will only cost about $50,000,000"

The grinch threw a party for him and all of his friends with all of the stuff he stole.

Why You Should Never Play Hide-n-seek
by Madison Hol

Pearl is waiting for her friends by a coral reef by her home. Since she is a mermaid she can't go on land. She is very disappointed, because she very much wants to go up on land and play with them up there. She is being approached by incoming strangers.

"Where in the world could they be? Oh, hi there! I'm just waiting for my friends. By the way my name is Pearl, and my friends' names are as followed: Uni the unicorn, who very much likes to speak in her native language Unicorn (she can actually talk in English, but she doesn't like to), Gardy the garden gnome, who is very outgoing, and Daisy the fairy, who is very shy. I'm just waiting for them to show up. Oh! Here they come!"

"Hey Pearl, who are you talking to?"

"Hey Gardy. Hey Uni. Hey Daisy. I'm just telling these very nice people what I was doing."

"Um, Pearl, Uni wants to know if we are going to play hide-n-seek," asked Daisy.

"No! Never again! Why? Oh! Let's tell them why! It all started when… hey did I tell you what mythical creature that I am? No? Well that shows you how forgetful I am, any way I'm a mermaid. Any way on with the story. It all started when I was waiting for my friends right around here, we were going to play hide-n-seek…"

"Where are they?"

"Hi Pearl!"

"Hi!

"Ready? OK! Let's go!"

'1,2,3,4,5,6,7,8,9,10,11,12,13,14,15,16,17,18,19,20,' I counted, 'Ready or not here I come!'

'Where are they? Uh-Oh! Maybe they got kidnapped by a sea monster! I've heard that there have been lots reports of weird activity over by Fisherman's Cove. I'd better go find them!'

~*~

THREE HOURS LATER

'Found them! Uh-Oh! I've been spotted!'

'I will get you little mermaid!'

'She has a name you know Mister Sea Monster, it's Pearl!'

'Seriously Gardy!?!'

'I have a name to you know, Miss Gnome, it's Salty!'

'Sorry! I forget important things sometimes, like not telling strangers any personal information! Oh! That's what I just did I'm terrible at remembering things. Great I did it again! And by the way I am not just any gnome, I am a garden gnome, Salty! Hey did I tell you that there are many different types of gnomes?'

'Oh, this is just great!'

'Ack! I've been caught!'

'It is impossible to get out of here, so don't even try,' said Salty right in my face, and let me tell you- his breath stunk horribly!'

'I'm out! Finally.'

'What about us?'

'I'll get you out, don't worry!'

'How do I get them out? Oh! I know!'

~*~

LATER THAT NIGHT

'I'd better hurry, I don't know how heavy he sleeps,' I said."

'I'm here, but be very quiet. I will get you out with the key so that we can lock the monster up in his own cave.'

'Great, thanks Pearl!'

'Neigh, neigh!'

'Uni says 'Thank you!' but I say 'this is bad!'

'Why Daisy?'

'Just look behind you and you'll find out.'

"Uh-Oh the sea monster! Quick lock him up!'

"And that is just what we did, lock him up."

~*~

TEN YEARS LATER

What Pearl didn't know was that she was going to get captured by Salty again.

"Oh, I wonder where they could be?" called out Daisy, for she had overcome her shyness.

Just as Daisy was calling that Pearl was being captured by Salty, and being taken to his hidden cave in the very deep part in the ocean.

"Now I've found everyone but Pearl." said Daisy, "Where do you guys think she could be?"

"Maybe Salty captured her again, let's go look by his cave," suggested Gardy.

"This is bad, Salty is guarding Pearl!" cried Daisy, "I guess we will have to do just what Pearl did, wait 'till night time rolls around again."

~*~

LATER THAT NIGHT

"Quick grab the key Uni!" cried Gardy.

"Neigh, neigh, neigh, neigh!"

That probably meant something like 'I am, just be quiet so we don't wake up Salty!' or, 'I'm hungry, so let's just get this done quickly.'

"Where are they? Oh! There they are!"

"Sorry Pearl. It took us a little while to find that key."

"It's OK."

"I got out and we put Salty in his cave and made sure that there were a lot more locks on it to make sure he couldn't get out. And that is why we will never again play hide-n-seek, because it just seems dangerous for us to play it."

"Yup. So we will all ways play tag- never ever hide-n-seek, and I recommend that you never play it either. 'Because you might just get kidnapped like we did."

"Gardy, don't scare them out of playing hide-n-seek," said Pearl "Just recommend it."

"Fine, but I just really don't want them to get kidnapped by a sea monster," said Gardy.

"Both of you stop, I think both of you forgot that they can't get kidnapped by a sea monster if they aren't in the sea, so just stop fighting before you scare them off. Okay?" reasoned Daisy.

"Fine, whatever you say Daisy."

"Fine, can we just start playing tag already?"

"Sure, I was just going to suggest that. Do you guys want to play to? Come on don't be shy."

~*~

"Bye, see you tomorrow! Have a good night!"

"Bye Pearl, you have a good night, too!"

"Bye Pearl"

"Neigh!"

"Oh, Uni why can't you just use English, like everyone else?"

"Well Unicorn is my native language, so it's just easier for me to."

"Ha! Made you speak English!"

"Oh, Pearl! You're such a trickster!"

"Made you do it again!"

"Stop it guys! Let's go Uni, before we run out of air."

"Okay, bye, Pearl."

And they lived happily ever after for a long time.

"Wait!" cried Pearl, "Before you go Daisy needs to tell me why she isn't wearing the chain of daisies that she always wears! Will you please tell me?"

"Fine! It's because I was in a hurry to get out of the house and pick up Uni, and why did you need to know?"

"'Because you never leave the house without your daisies!"

"THE END!" cried all the friends safe and sound away from Salty the Sea Monster who is locked in his cave in his in the dark depths of the ocean away from any curious mermaid or fish in the area at just the wrong time. It would be bad if he got out, and took out his anger on them and they got locked in his cave all alone scared and worried that they will never get out again. But they would probably get out anyway no matter what Salty said about never getting out again because it is a very weak cave so they would probably get out very quickly.

The Dent in the Jungle

by Laurey Johnson

I really hate rain. Rain in my hair. Rain in my boots. Rain in my clothes. It's soaked me through and through. My hair looks brown instead of blonde. My freckles are more numerous than before. My short body looks like a stub in the mud. The only things that look remotely human on me are my legs. Well, at least one leg. My good one. My fake one can't grasp mud on its hairless surface.

I am, or was, a good animal rescuer. My job for the past 2 years has been to move the tigers from the Sumatra Jungle in Indonesia, to the safer plains in South Africa. And it has gone so terribly wrong.

It's not just my leg. It's my dipstick of a co-worker right next to me. Bob Stonewall is the one who stole my job. He is now the popular hero, and I'm left here in the dust of my own crippled-ness.

"Troop!" yelled Mr. Jack. "We can't get through to the cub by walking. Somebody scramble up that tree. Now!"

"I'll do it!" I yelled back to him.

"Don't worry about it partner, I can do it instead." replied Bob

"But-"

"No time! Get your butt up that tree!" interrupted Mr. Jack.

I screamed internally. Mr. Jack was a nice guy, (since he paid us), but sometimes he was intolerable.

"I'm going up that tree no matter what!" I shouted.

I was almost to the base of the tree when Luke picked me up. Luke is a very quiet guy. Nobody knows much about him, and I haven't made much of an effort.

"Let me go, ya creep!"

"Flow," said Mr. Jack. "you can't plunge headlong into something dangerous."

"But sir, it's just climbing up a wet tree to grab a scaredy-cat."

"James, one more word out of you and you'll be suspended." screamed Mr. Jack. "Besides, Bob just got the cub. It would've fallen because you couldn't get there fast enough."

Luke put me down. Without looking behind me, I started slowly toward the camp. I couldn't help hearing the cheers of the crew behind me.

I got to camp only 5 minutes before the others. Mr. Jack announced that there would be a big supper tonight in honor of Bob. I started walking towards my tent, when Luke stopped me.

"I'm sorry about, um, harshly using force to lift you off the ground, it's just that-" Luke was interrupted by Bob.

"Hey Flow, how's it going?" he asked coolly.

"Rotten, thanks to you, of course." I replied hotly.

"That's too bad because everybody but you seem to adore me and my great heroism."

Luke muttered something under his breath.

"Excuse me but I have to go," said Bob. "I've got a feast waiting for me."

I turned around and left him and Luke in the dust. I stared at my left leg and blamed it for all my problems. I also blamed the rain that continuously washed away my dreams into the forest.

I waited until everyone had gone through supper, and took the scraps. I am pretty sure that that dude Bob is trying to ruin my life. I also think that there is something off about the person. I feel like the loss of my left leg was a gain to him. Right before I lost it, I saw him there watching his watch nervously...

"Hey," said Luke. "do you want to play a game of card poacher?"

Card poacher is my favorite game. I've gotten really good at it due to life problems.

"Ok. I'll deal first."

We played for thirty minutes. We chatted a bit and learned about each other's lives. Luke is apparently a sore loser. All conversation about my leg was avoided. I was about to call it a night when Luke asked, "What happened to your leg? I hear so many stories about you venturing to do something stupid or, um, reckless."

"Let me guess, you heard them from Bob. And Mr. Jack. And all of the other buffoons who sit around and wait for their hero to save the day."

"Um, ok. Anyways, what really happened?"

I sighed. Telling this story was like reliving the end of my life. I started speaking to Luke, and the nightmare began.

Last year, I was considered the team's hero. I was always ready to jump into action, to ride by the seat of my pants, type of person. But of course, that was also the year that Bob became my partner. We were on a duo mission in the heart of the vast jungle. This part of the jungle was bright green, it's leaves all covered with rain from the last storm. The birds were singing as usual, their bright melody, lifting my spirits up. Bob and I had to capture a male tiger that was 360lbs, he was massive and could overtake us easily. That's why Mr. Jack gave me this job, I knew what I was doing.

"Bob," I had said, "Get the tranquilizer gun ready and loaded."

"You got it Flow." He replied.

He took the gun and aimed for the tiger. I noticed that the tranquilizer dart was only half-full. He was about to pull the trigger, (also the trigger to the end of my left leg).

"Stop!" I yelled, but it was too late.

The tiger turned at the sound of my voice. The dart nicked his ear, driving it into a further rage. The birds stopped singing. Right before the tiger jumped me, I saw Bob check his watch. I felt crushed under the immense weight of the tiger's body. Then I knew nothing.

When I came to, I was in a hospital. I looked at my leg and saw that it was gone. I looked under the blanket again and again. My leg was nowhere to be found. Some doctors told me that my leg had to be removed in order to survive. I thanked them for helping me, but all I could think of was the reality of my missing limb.

I obviously didn't tell Luke my feelings in detail, but I could feel them in my retelling of my story.

Mr. Jack came rushing in the dining hall. He said, "We need to have a team meeting now. Our research crew found some suspicious activity around the center of the jungle."

Our research crew is another aspect of our mission. They watch and track the tigers' habits, diet, and movement to ensure that they will survive once they reach African plains. They usually research during the day, but once a week they will go out in the night since tigers are nocturnal animals.

We made it to the meeting tent 5 minutes early. Other team members were filing in, when an unfamiliar face walked in the tent. Two policemen were right behind him. Was he a poacher? And if so, shouldn't he be in a courthouse or a prison?

"Members of Team Sumatra," said Mr. Jack, "as none of you know until now, the tigers have been disappearing in far more numbers this week than the last week."

Nervous murmurs passed through the team. Mr. Jack continued.

"Our researchers hadn't a clue until Bob found a hunter's shack in the center of the jungle."

Applause pelted the room.

"And," finished Mr. Jack, "this man."

More nervous murmurs filled the room. The police held him with a tight grip around his shoulders.

Then the bigger policeman spoke, "We have caught the thug, but we can't bring him to the jail, it's at least 50 miles from here, and our car broke down. There may be a whole band of poachers, so keep an eye out."

"Also," said the second policeman, "we need a volunteer to help keep the prisoner secure in a tent. Any volunteers?"

Of course Bob volunteered. I saw it coming. If he was to keep his heroic reputation, he had to do everything to keep it up. I went to my tent, and flopped onto my bed. I could hear my tent-mates chatting about tonight, and the strange poacher man who appeared. It was going to be a long night.

The Next Day...

The man was gone. Totally gone. Irreplaceably gone. Bob claims that he had been knocked out. I didn't believe a word of his story, so I said, "Prove it."

"Prove it?" Bob asked. "Prove my loyalty that you already know I have? Prove the trustworthiness that I've already displayed? Why would you dare-"

"Prove it." I said again.

"I uh-"

"He doesn't have to prove anything, Flow. You know what a hero he's been to us. Just because you are jealous, doesn't mean you can treat him any different than before." said Mr. Jack.

"But sir, I'm-"

"Not interested. That tongue of yours is liable to get you fired. Just be glad that I saved your skin."

With that, everyone dispersed into their mission groups. I went with my group to search areas where the last tigers had been seen. We gathered supplies and went out. Luke gave me a 'thumbs up' before we progressed further on the trail. I smiled back. He was helping the policemen fix their car. I turned my attention back towards the trail.

Along the way, I saw another shack. I panicked for a moment, until I realized it was Bob's shack. I saw something orange. Lying on the ground was a dead tiger. It was very young too. I looked very carefully and found a wound right where its heart is. A dead tiger next to Bob's shack. The strange man escaping under Bob's surveillance. Bob not proving his unconsciousness. Bob must be helping the poachers. Bob must be using his heroism as a cover for his poaching.

"Gu-" a hand covered my mouth. The poacher that had escaped, had his hand over my mouth.

The strange man carried me into Bob's shack. I've only been here once, when I helped him build the shack. The man tied me to a sturdy beam in the center of the shack. He then started to whistle and sing, "Zebadiah, do, do, do. You are the best, do, do, do. You caught the girl, do, do, do. Like Bob said to, to, to!"

Just then Bob walked in the room. He had a tiger skin with him.

"Oh Flow, I can explain," said Bob cautiously. "I found this-"

"I know your plan, bozo. You hired the dummy next to me to hunt tigers and kill them for, um, for-"

"Money of course. Didn't you know that the finest skins came from here? I make over a million dollars with just one dead tiger. Amazing how I can use death for my gain."

"Listen here psychopath, if you kill all the tigers here, you can't sell anymore furs."

"True. But I could still make a large sum of money."

"Ok. But when Mr. Jack figures out what you did Stonewall -"

"Mr. Jack will not find out. I will make sure of that. He totally trusts me. And as for you, I will find a way to keep you from talking." He thought for a while. Then a smirk came across his face. "Would you like to lose your other leg, James? I can see it now. The poacher comes and stabs your leg, rendering you utterly helpless. Then you will be removed, and I will continue my secret operation." He took 3 knives from his pockets. I started breathing heavily. He threw the knives, all three at once onto my left leg, I could barely hide my expression from Bob. Then I saw nothing.

I opened my eyes and smiled. Bob was definitely still a dipstick. He threw the knives into the wrong leg. I listened to make sure they were both out of earshot. I heard nothing but the usual animal sounds like the birds… I don't hear the birds. This is really bad. The birds only stop singing if there is danger nearby. In this jungle it meant tigers. I quickly grabbed one of the knives and started to cut the ropes. I heard a creak and then-

"Flow!" shouted Luke in surprise. "Where have you been? Oh my gosh, are those knives in your leg?"

"It was Bob," I said, "and the man who escaped. Bob is no hero! He's just using this job to cover up his poaching activities! We've got to go stop them!"

"I know where they are." Luke replied. "Bob came to camp 30 minutes ago and told us that you had gone missing. He sent out the search parties and stayed behind at the camp; he said poachers might be lurking near."

"He wasn't lying when he said that." muttered to myself. "Let's go to camp now. He might already be making his get-away."
I ran as fast as I could, which was getting me nowhere, considering that my peg leg didn't help one bit.

"May I harshly handle you again?" Luke asked sheepishly.

"Shut up, pick me up, and run up to the camp with all your might." I rolled my eyes at him.

We made it to camp just in time to see Bob drive away in the police vehicle. Luke ran and rushed at the vehicle. But it was hopeless, they had gotten away. I scanned the road and saw a tiger with a torn ear. Holy. Cow. It was THE tiger, (the one that had demolished my leg), that was right in front of me. In a way though, this cat actually saved my life.

He stopped right in front of Bob's car. Bob hit the brakes and just missed the tiger. The tiger crouched in a pouncing pose. It leaped off its giant hind legs, when *Thump*. It landed on the ground. I had shot it with my tranquilizer gun.

I approached Bob carefully, tranq gun in front of me. He stepped out of the car with his hands up. He saw the gun in my hand. "You could've killed me." he said. "But you didn't. You let me live. Why, annoying peasant?"

I replied, "A life is a life, no matter who it came from." Luke picked him up and hauled him to the policemen. They took their car and Bob and left the camp. I hope I never see that dude again.

5 Years Later...

I could feel the warmth of the African plains before we left the airport. The tiger had all been successfully moved, and in the nick of time too. Right on the last day 2050, Sumatra's Jungle flooded due to heavy rainfall. The tigers' living spaces had been completely destroyed.

Now they were all safe in South Africa. I looked down and saw my peg leg. It still had its dent from the knife in the jungle. I breathed the warm afternoon air and sighed. It gave me the feeling of life; the life I had worked so hard to preserve.

Random Stories

Monopoly

by Erica De Bruin

Marie and Annie are best friends. Marie was at Annie's house playing Monopoly with her when Annie's little brother barged into her bedroom.

"I want to play!" John said.

"Come on let's go to the woods." Annie said to Marie.

Since Annie lived by the woods they went there a lot. They were sad that they couldn't finish their Monopoly game. They were walking through the woods when they came across a mansion. The mansion was gorgeous and humongous. We went to the door and knocked on it. A nice elderly lady came to the door and welcomed us in.

"Hello there." said the lady. "My name is Rose what is your guys' name?"

"Well, I'm Marie and this is my best friend Annie." said Marie

Rose had just made chocolate chip cookies that smelled REALLY REALLY good. She let us have one that tasted just as good as it smelled. When we were done with our snack we were going to leave, but Rose asked if we wanted to play a game. We couldn't say no to her she was just too nice.

"What games do you have?" The girls asked.

"Well let's see here, I have Ticket to Ride, Candyland, The Farming Game, a deck cards, and Monopoly." she said

We were so excited to hear that she had Monopoly. We spent the rest of the afternoon playing Monopoly, eating cookies and hearing stories about her beautiful house. By the way Rose is very good at Monopoly she won both times we played. It was getting dark, so we started heading home to Annie's house. It was supper time when we got home. We were having chicken and rice. Marie had to go home after supper, but every day after school we went over to the gorgeous, humongous house to visit Rose, eat chocolate chip cookies and play the all-time favorite game Monopoly.

The Legend of Drakon

by Eli Hoksbergen

The company of men, dwarves, and elves placed their orders at The Happy Horse at the base of the Athsunian Mountains. The leader, a man named Rorain said, "We need a plan." Just as Jhim the Elf was going to respond, the two waiters bearing the heavily laden trays entered the room and asked if they were ready to eat. They were, and once the food had been served, eaten, and cleaned up, they resumed their conversation with Rorain standing and heavily leaning on his carved wooden staff.

"Here is the plan as I see it. First we send an invitation to the dwarf, Garsvog, telling him to meet us at Argent where we meet Dealon. We then proceed to the Gray Lands. Once we have crossed them, we can rent a boat across the White Sound, and then to the Mountains of Fire. But first, to bed so we can get an early rise tomorrow." With a shout the company left the room, and charged down the hall in the direction of their beds.

The next day the company loaded up the horses with their saddlebags and set off on the path of Darshima, the road to Argent. As the horses plodded along, Orok and Jhim were the rear guard, while Rorain took up the lead. About an hour later, the company was ambushed by a trio of goblins, which greatly troubled them because goblins had not been seen since the Great War.

The next thirteen days passed uneventfully, and so, on the fourteenth day of their trek they reached Argent. They found the tavern The Dancing Dragon and ordered a brief luncheon. They ate it, and when they were done set out to the Castle of Thangmar, where Garsvog of the family of Durgrimst Horthbirust lived. Returning to the Dancing Dragon, they waited for the mage Dealon to show up.

That night, while Rorain was in bed, a ship woven of grass and about two feet long bumped into his window. He quietly rose, so as not to wake the others, and crept over to the window and opened it. After a second, Rorain saw a tiny piece of paper stuck to one of the masts. He carefully took the note and read it.

Dear Rorain and company,

    I am sorry I cannot meet you in person at Argent. I am being followed. I am already on the road and will meet you shortly after you leave the town.

    May the stars watch over you

    Dealon W. Witmmon

    The next morning, they left The Dancing Dragon early and meet with Dealon. To everyone's surprise and delight, he conjured up a magic portal which took them straight to the Mountain of Fire. There they met the dragon, Drakon, got his autograph, and made it home safely back to their families without any more incidents.

The Girl and Her Goose Egg

by Madison Hol

Once upon a time there was a girl that had a big goose egg on her head.

"Oh! Hi there! My name is Isabella, don't tell anyone, but I am that girl. Let me tell you how I got it.

I was just sitting there under my apple tree and someone came up to me gagged me, tied me up, and threw me into the back of their truck! I tried to scream, but my efforts proved useless- remember, I was gagged- I also tried to kick, but that was useless, too. Once we got to our destination I realized that we were at an abandoned hotel and I thought that they were going to put me in one of the rooms and leave me there until someone ransomed me out, but luckily they didn't. I was terrified and didn't know if I would ever get out and see my family again! I got hit on the head three times- once when they were putting me in the truck, another time when they were taking me out, and when they were taking me into the hotel. It turns out that the hotel was their hideout, and they were going to keep me as their servant to cook and clean for them. If I ever wanted to see my parents again I would have to get out, and quick. I really did hope that I would get out before the next day, but I did not, I ended up getting out the next Tuesday night while they were still sleeping and I have not seen them yet again, and I hope that I never do. When I got back home I still had the big goose egg and my parents asked me what happened and I told them that I had gotten kidnapped and that I had hit my head three times. That's it. Oh, I have to go sorry. Bye!"

The Door in the Wall

by Laurey Johnson

Nellie Anderson woke up and rubbed her brown eyes. Another boring day. She combed through her brown hair and sighed. Nothing ever happened to her. She was an average, American 14-year old. She woke up at 7:00 every day, got ready for school, and left for school at 7:30, every day. She brushed her teeth and took a shower. She got dressed and packed for school. She went down stairs and yelled, "Bye Mom!"

Nellie was about to walk out the door when she heard a knock. "Mom, were you expecting someone?" Nellie asked. When no one answered, she searched the house for her mother. She was not there. Someone knocked on the door again.

"Who is it?" said Nellie cautiously. Still no one answered. Nellie was getting nervous. "Mom!" she whispered harshly. Still no answer. She decided that she would try asking who was at the door again.

"Who is it? Okay, if you don't answer I'm not going to-"

The door exploded into a million pieces. A man stepped through the debris. "Get her!" He shouted to his men, "And don't let her escape!"

Nellie froze as a swarm of men rushed at her. They had machine guns and camo clothes. They wore sunglasses and army helmets. They almost reached her.

Then Nellie remembered were she was, and bolted through the living room. She rushed up the stairs, throwing furniture behind her. She made it to the top floor, were there were to rooms and the attic. She rushed up to her ancient attic, determining that it was the easiest hiding spot.

Just as locked the attic door, the men made it up the stairs. She overheard one of them saying, "Where did she go? Is it that hard to find a 14-year old girl? Remember, you idiots, she is dangerous! She could destroy America! Do you want that?"

A chorus of "No" echoed through the floor.

"Then get moving!!" the man screeched.

Nellie was dumbstruck. How could she possibly be dangerous? She had never done anything wrong in her life. Except for telling a few lies here and there, anyone could tell you that she had done no wrong.

"Check the attic!" a man shouted.

Nellie looked around and darted for a closet in the corner.

How do I get out of here? She thought to herself. She was trapped.

Just then a door appeared in the closet.

"What the-" a crack sounded from the door." I don't what the heck this is," she breathed, "but it looks better than what's going on with those strange men."

She opened the door and jumped through it. What she saw changed her life. There was a box with a lock on it. It had an inscription that said, "Open the box, or lie forever in wonder of what's inside." Nellie stared at it for a long time. Finally, she got the courage to open. "Wait," she said to herself, "I don't have a key. How will I ever open this?" A key fell from nowhere and landed at her feet.

"Guess that solves my problems."

She approached the chest very slowly. She shoved the key into the lock and turned it. Nothing happened.

"It probably had noth-"

BAAM. The chest exploded. Nellie stared in horror at what was inside. There was a yellowish-red glowing light emanating from the remains of the chest. It made a low humming sound that was somewhat hypnotizing.

Nellie got up and started walking towards it. She had no clue what she was doing, but she REALLY wanted to touch it. She almost touched it, then pulled back.

"I can't touch it. I don't know what it will do to me." She turned around and started walking away. "But I have to know what it is!"

She ran back and put her finger on it. Instantly it rushed inside her and lit up her entire body. She looked at her palm and the picture of a flame formed there. Her hair got a red streak in in it, and her eyes were now red.

She closed her eyes. When she opened them, she was back in her closet. The men were almost to the door. They started shooting at her, but they couldn't. She waved her hand and pushed them all back. All but one of them ran away. It was the man that was their leader.

"I am General Foster and the American government will get you, Nellie. You're too dangerous to live."

"That may be so," replied Nellie, "but you I'm not Nellie anymore. I'm Solar Eclipse!"

With that, she moved her hands towards him, and he went flying. She let out a sigh of relief. She was satisfied. They were gone. But now, her life would never be the same. She had to leave. She needed to find her mother. She left the house and said, "Time to really live."

www.ingramcontent.com/pod-product-compliance
Lightning Source LLC
Chambersburg PA
CBHW060501010526
44118CB00018B/2490